ideals
CHRISTMAS

W9-BSB-543

Keep Thou our hearts, we humbly pray,
Free from all greed this Christmas Day:
Fill us with love, and grant that we
Be clad with Christ's humility.

Place in the manger of the mind
The gift of love for all mankind.
Leave in the homes of every kin
Joy—and "Peace on earth, goodwill to men!"

Stella Craft Tremble

ISBN 0-8249-1066-4

Publisher, Patricia A. Pingry
Executive Editor, Peggy Schaefer
Art Director, Patrick McRae
Production Manager, Jan Johnson
Associate Editor, Joan Anderson
Editorial Assistant, Kathleen Gilbert
Copy Editor, Becky Maginn

Front and back covers from Bob Taylor Photography

Inside back cover by Ed Cooper

IDEALS—Vol. 45, No. 8 December MCMLXXXVIII IDEALS (ISSN 0019-137X) is published eight times a year,
February, March, May, June, August, September, November, December
by IDEALS PUBLISHING CORPORATION, Nelson Place at Elm Hill Pike, Nashville, Tenn. 37214
Second class postage paid at Nashville, Tennessee, and additional mailing offices.
Copyright © MCMLXXXVIII by IDEALS PUBLISHING CORPORATION.
POSTMASTER: Send address changes to Ideals, Post Office Box 148000, Nashville, Tenn. 37214-8000
All rights reserved. Title IDEALS registered U.S. Patent Office.

SINGLE ISSUE—$3.95
ONE-YEAR SUBSCRIPTION—eight consecutive issues as published—$17.95
TWO-YEAR SUBSCRIPTION—sixteen consecutive issues as published—$31.95
Outside U.S.A., add $6.00 per subscription year for postage and handling.

The Red Leaves and the Green

Nadine Brothers Lybarger

A splash of vibrant color
Upon the Christmas scene
Are beautiful poinsettias
With the red leaves and the green.

So brilliant in their blooming;
Small gemlike flowers unfold
To crown their loveliness of leaf
With gleaming red and gold.

In a sea of decorations,
They add that special touch
Of a living, glowing atmosphere
That always means so much.

When we think of the poinsettias,
We think of Christmas cheer
And beauty that stays with us
Far into the coming year.

Photo Overleaf
KARWENDEL RANGE
AUSTRIA
M. Thonig
H. Armstrong Roberts, Inc.

Photo Opposite
MITCHELL PARK HORTICULTURAL CONSERVATORY
MILWAUKEE, WISCONSIN
Ken Dequaine

Snow

Anton J. Stoffle

The snowflakes glisten as they fall,
And soon the snow will cover all;

Like nature's blanket silky white,
Snow tends to cleanse and make things bright.

Each rooftop sports its fine new coat;
They're all well covered, none to gloat,

As trees with branches rough and bare
Wear sleeves against the winter air.

The fluffs and puffs that blow about,
So picturesque, draw children out;

A sled, a snowman, or such things,
With sounds of laughter snowtime brings.

A snarl of traffic when snow's deep
Can land one in a jolly heap.

But setting all such things aside,
Just watch the youngsters with great pride,

Recalling days of long ago,
When we all played out in the snow;

Oh, how we sledded, jumped, and rolled
In fallen snow, despite the cold.

Somehow we cross the span of years,
Forgetting worries, cares, and fears,

When we sit and watch the falling snow
And let the flakes just drift and blow.

Photo Opposite
SNOW-CLAD HILLSIDES
DANE COUNTY, WISCONSIN
Ken Dequaine

Lodestar

God put the stars in the Christmas sky
And then chose the brightest one
To shine upon the manger rough
Where lay his newborn son.

The silent star the darkness broke,
Spreading brilliance from above,
Covering the earth with glory as
It shone on the Prince of Love.

It was the lodestar of three wise men,
Guiding them on their way.
They followed it unto Bethlehem town,
To where the baby lay.

Jeanne Seaman
Yucaipa, CA

The Sounds of Christmas

Which of us can ere forget
The sounds of Christmas telling yet
Of all those special times we had
With brothers, sisters, Mom, and Dad;

The "oohs" and "aahs" of sweet surprise
Accompanied by sparkling eyes
When gifts were opened Christmas morn
Amidst the sounds of paper torn;

The squeal of unmistaken joy
Expelled with each and every toy;
The crunch of newly fallen snow
On crystal nights, at ten below.

And who among us can't recall,
When things were quiet after all,
The sigh of satisfaction felt
When Dad sat back, with an open belt;

The crackling of a burning log
While parents sipped a glass of nog;
And in the dinner's aftermath
The moans and groans of stomach's wrath.

So listen with a careful ear
When Christmas comes again this year,
For all around you, day and night,
Are wondrous sounds of new delight.

And later on in Autumn's years,
When all-pervasive quiet nears,
The sounds of Christmas evermore
Will be right there, in memory's store.

Thomas G. DiMuro
Garden Grove, CA

Reflections

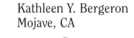

Christmas in Florida

When poinsettias are afire,
My heart no longer holds desire
For frozen lakes and drifted snow
In zero weather, or below.
I now have reached the tender age
That watches winter's weather gauge
And turns the electric blanket high
Whenever there's a leaden sky
That chills the wind and veils the sun.
These sunny seasons make me one
Remembering the fireside cheer
Of youthful days—yet holding dear
The warmth of nature's solar heat
That turns an orange honey-sweet.

Beatrice Branch
Miami, FL

Not Sent To

It always happens just to me
At this time every year.
Despite the planning on my part,
It's what I always fear.

I've signed and sealed and mailed my cards
And soaked my aching wrist.
I've heaved a sigh of great relief.
I've finished up the list.

And then, when all my cards are mailed,
It's almost always true:
The very next day I get a card
From someone NOT sent to!

Kathleen Y. Bergeron
Mojave, CA

Editor's Note: Readers are invited to submit unpublished, original poetry, short anecdotes, and humorous reflections on life for possible publication in future *Ideals* issues. Please send copies only; manuscripts will not be returned. Writers will receive $10 for each published submission. Send materials to "Readers' Reflections," Ideals Publishing Corporation, Nelson Place at Elm Hill Pike, Nashville, Tennessee 37214.

Once Again We Pause

Lucile E. Teske

Whatever else we lose throughout the years,
Let us keep Christmas, shining and apart,
And cast aside grim worries and dark fears
To feel a stir of joy within the heart.

If dreams have failed and disappointments throng
While problems seem too difficult to face,
The muted cadence of the angels' song
Renews again this blessed time of grace.

Unrest and folly, glimmerings of war
Enmesh us in a net of puzzling strife,
But far above the Star still goes before
To point the way to happiness and life.

May hearts be listening when the joy bells ring
New courage, faith, and hope on Christmas morn,
As once again we pause, remembering
That unto us the Prince of Peace is born.

COLLECTOR'S CORNER

Trains from the collection of Albert Ruocchio

Toy trains occupy a small place in the whole world of collectible toys. As a group, however, toy train enthusiasts are probably exceeded in numbers only by doll collectors.

Collecting toy trains must be separated clearly from scale model railroading. Toy trains were, and are, made to be played with, to make noise and entertain the young. Scale models are for the advanced modeler, who recreates in his home a real railroad to scale, with schedules and routines of operation. As the technology of manufacturing toy trains improved, it gave birth to the scale trains.

Even today's scale model enthusiasts, though, got their start with a toy train and a simple loop of track. There is hardly a father or grandfather today who can walk away from a toy train display and not be nostalgic about his youth. Collector and author Louis Hertz has said that a new enthusiast will always seek first those trains that were made at the time he or she was thirteen to fourteen years old. How true! Time and time again I see it not only in my own collecting, but also in the collecting of my friends and acquaintances.

The great toy train makers—Harry Ives (Ives Trains), Joshua Lionel Cowan (Lionel Trains), William O. Coleman (American Flyer, Chicago), Louis Marx (Marx Trains), Alfred C. Gilbert (American Flyer, New Haven), etc.—not only produced wonderful trains for generations of children, but they also did a tremendous job of selling those trains from the turn of the century to the midsixties. Those of us who lived through the heyday of toy trains remember our great anticipation in waiting for catalogs that would show the sets and pieces to be sold each new "train year." The catalogs usually were issued in the late summer or early fall, always well in advance of the yearly trip to see Santa, or, as we grew older, in time for good hints to be left for our parents. These catalogs were our treasures and the dream books of our youth.

Today the same catalogs are sources of information for train collecting. They should never be considered the last word on the existence of a particular item in a particular color or with a particular lettering, since economic factors and changes in production runs created differences between the catalog listings and that which was actually produced. Color, printing, and layout variations are plentiful; after all, yesterday's manufacturers were simply building toys for children. These manufacturers could not have foreseen how frustrating the differences would be to today's collectors who aspire to own everything of a specific make or category.

Lionel standard gauge, circa 1937

Still, it is a pleasure today to read these catalogs and dream of the days when we could visit the department stores or the local hardware store, watch the trains running while our parents were busy with other Christmas surprises, and even purchase beautifully created toy copies of the mammoths of the rails.

Toy trains are divided into numerous classifications. Three major categories are cast-iron pull trains, windup trains (domestic and foreign), and electric trains.

Electric trains form the largest category, as mass production techniques virtually flooded the market with these toys. The two major subcategories are pre-World War II and post-World War II trains. The prewar

Lionel Spirit of 1776, manufactured in honor of the bicentennial

trains are categorized by manufacturer, age, and rail gauge. The two major gauges are O gauge and standard gauge: O gauge trains run on tracks where outside rails are 1¼ inches apart, while the much larger standard gauge trains run on track with a rail separation almost twice that of O gauge.

Toy train origins are easy to identify, since the manufacturer is clearly marked on each piece, usually on the bottom. Every engine, car, piece, or accessory also has a number, clearly imprinted on both sides or on its base. Collectors can hold enthusiastic discussions about trains, just by exchanging numbers. For example, one might call his friend and tell him that he has just acquired a Lionel 700E, a 381, and a blue 400E with the cars. At the end of that call, the listener would either be pleased for his friend or jealous, depending upon whether or not those items were already in his collection.

To exchange information and the trains themselves, the Train Collectors Association (TCA) was created in 1954. Originally there were only two small chapters, in Pennsylvania and California. Now there are more than 19,500 members worldwide. Why this love of trains and the strength of an organization like TCA? It all goes back to our youth and our love of the little toy replica of the real iron horse traversing a small oval of track under our Christmas tree.

Albert Ruocchio

Winter Fishing

Helen Fahrbach

Here come the fishermen back from the shanties
That huddle far out on the ice-covered lake,
Trudging in boot prints that pattern the snow crust,
Breath trailing plumes in a frosty white wake.

Boys follow fathers with light-footed leaping,
They frolic and tumble in sport of their own;
Shouting and laughing they climb up the hillside,
Fathers and sons, icy cold and windblown.

Bringing in winter, wild wind, and snow flurries,
Their boots, caps, and mittens they drop in a heap;
Home are the fishermen, both generations,
Leaving the fish swimming safe in the deep.

Song of the Ski Jump

Minnie Klemme

There's a singing of wind, and muscle, and brain;
There's a power, directed and free;
There's a magic which only the skyborne attain
Gliding along on their skis.

There's a singing of seconds clearing the slope;
There's a moment of breath in the air;
There's a gliding so swift that one never need grope
For a landing that isn't quite there.

There's a singing of wood, a singing of steel;
There's a thrill one cannot define.
There's a surging of pulses no heart can conceal
When the skier comes straight down the line.

Pine Trees on a Silky Road

Marion Schoeberlein

Pine trees on a silky road
Are sometimes nature's poems;
I wonder who will buy them now
And put them in their homes
To scent their parlors with perfume,
An angel at the top.
Pine trees along a silky road
Make me want to stop
And just remember Christmases
Of decades long ago,
When there was lots of caroling,
And people in the snow,
Stopped for merry Christmas greetings—
It was a world that glowed.
Thank God for memories that come
With pine trees on a silky road.

Country Chronicle

Lansing Christman

December colors the hills and valleys with an array of Christmas hues: the festive green and red, the silver, the white, and the gold.

We had our Yuletide hues in the North, not far from the Helderbergs in upstate New York. Now we have them in the South, in the Blue Ridge foothills of South Carolina. At this time of year, dramatic colors are everywhere—near the doorstep, in the marsh and woodland, and on the banks of purling streams. So vivid are the colors nature offers in this season that they instantly call up memories of Christmastimes long past.

The pine, spruce, cedar, magnolia, hemlock, and holly are the green. We need only lift a spray of hemlock bough and examine the undersides of the miniature needles to find the silver. The white surrounds us in freshly fallen snow.

Nandina berries range from deep orange to Christmasy red. Nandina may be found in the yard, or in the woods and along fencerows, where the seeds have been scattered by birds in some past year. Another traditional source of Yuletide red is the holly berry. In the North, the black alder, a member of the holly family, is a favorite because of its bright red berry clusters.

There can be a touch of gold in late-blossoming dandelions, almost hidden in the grass and weeds. They glow like nuggets in the December sun.

So dream for a while, if you will, and the magical colors of a Christmas countryside may sweep you home again on the wings of enduring memories, just as they do me.

Winter Countryside

Ada Mae Hoffrek

The winter winds blow from the North
As snow rides far and wide,
While nature lends a helping hand
To clothe the countryside.

The little trees and slender twigs
Dance 'round like dainty queens,
In party dress of purest white,
A winter wonder dream!

The flowers of spring have gone away,
No green on mountainside;
O'er all the hills the blanket fell . . .
Winter is far and wide.

Year after year the winds blow cold,
Bringing the snows so deep;
But curled up in their beds below
The little flowers sleep.

Photo Opposite
WINTER LANE
HADLYME, CONNECTICUT
Fred M. Dole Productions

Signs before Christmas

George W. Goretzke

Christmastime is drawing nearer,
I can see it in the sky;
I can tell it on the faces
Of the strangers passing by.
I can tell it in the quiet
When I go to bed at night,
And the sparkle of the flicker
In the fireplace, burning bright.

Christmas Eve's around the corner,
I can tell by Mother's eyes;
And the way she locks the closet
And her happy "aahs" and sighs.
I can tell it by the teacher,
When I slip and break a rule,
And the other kids around me
While we're on the way to school.

I can see it, I can tell it,
I can feel it drawing near
By the way my father whistles
And my sisters call me "dear."
And the way the house is cleaner,
With the old things put away;
I can tell it plain as spellin',
That old Santa's on his way.

Christmas Day is gettin' closer;
I'm as good as I can be
'Til the others start to wonder
What the world is wrong with me.
But I guess they don't remember
How it was in days of old
When the shepherds stood and listened
To the story angels told.

And I guess they just don't feel it
In the atmosphere at night,
When they say the tree's too gaudy
And the ornaments too bright.
But in little folks it's different,
When it's nearin' Christmas Day;
We can see it, we can hear it
When old Santa's on the way!

Dear Santa

Kathleen Monahan and Kathie Rizzo

I am writing this letter for my brother because his arm is in a sling, and the doctor said he shouldn't move his fingers too much. He sprained his wrist yesterday when he fell off the refrigerator, and we've all been pretty busy since then. My mother says it's amazing how putting one arm in a sling can keep three people jumping.

But my brother said he won't ask for anything else if I only write this letter to you to explain what he was doing on the refrigerator. He's afraid you'll forget about how good he's been for most of this year.

And, really, he has been pretty good. He's only had a few slip-ups. Like the time he painted Jerome. He and Jerome found the paints in a box in the garage, and I guess they figured they were watercolors and they'd wash right off. My brother was as surprised as anybody when Jerome's mother called to say that she could not get the green stars off Jerome's forehead. I don't think you should blame my brother for this because it was really just an accident, and the stars wore off in a couple of days.

My brother's really pretty good most of the time. He saved Mrs. Dougherty's cat when it got too high up in the tree. My mother said that she felt like fainting when she saw him climbing way out on that branch, but even she had to admit that he was trying to do a good thing.

My mother says his heart's in the right place, and he cares about other people. Once he gave a giant jar of olives to the school cafeteria. He won the olives at a carnival by guessing that there were 870 of them in the jar. He guessed it exactly. My father told him it was an amazing thing to do, but my brother said that he couldn't eat that many olives in a hundred years and could he give them to somebody that needed them. So my father brought them to the school and bought my brother and me ice cream sodas to celebrate.

You see, he's really pretty good, so I know you'll understand when I tell you about the refrigerator.

What started it was when my mother hid the Christmas cookies. She said she had to hide them because last year we only left some burned macaroons and she had to serve store-bought cookies on Christmas. So my brother and I decided to play detective. It was only a game. Really. I mean we weren't going to eat the cookies. We were just going to find them.

My brother was playing bloodhound and sniffing the air in the kitchen when, all of a sudden, he started barking and pointing at the cabinet over the refrigerator. He stood on the highchair and climbed up on the top of the refrigerator. When he opened the cabinet, the yelping got louder, and the next thing I knew he was on the floor, covered with chocolate chips and pecan sandies.

He wasn't worried about his hand so much as he was about getting the cookies back into the saltines boxes that my mother had hidden them in. So we picked them up real fast and didn't even eat one. We put them back in the boxes and cleaned up the crumbs, and that's when my mother came in and my brother's hand started to hurt.

So, you see, it was just a detective game that he was playing, and he wasn't trying to swipe the cookies. And it was pretty smart to guess that they were in the saltines boxes because he knew my mother knew that he doesn't like saltines any more than he likes olives.

So now that you know what happened, I know you'll decide to give my brother the things that he asked for and not hold it against him that he fell off the refrigerator in the middle of a game.

I hope that you do, Santa, 'cause he's really a pretty good brother most of the time. But, if I were you, I'd hold off on giving him the blowtorch for a while.

Painting Opposite
LETTER TO SANTA
John Slobodnik

The Carolers

Louise Dale Nelson

I read again on Christmas Eve
How prophets had foretold
The coming of the Prince of Peace,
And I saw the scene unfold.
Out in the fields with the shepherds,
Lost in sorcery's spell,
I hushed my steps to lend an ear
To catch the first noel.

I saw the town of Bethlehem,
Heard glad hosannas sing,
"Glory to God in the highest,
All hail the newborn King."
Then as the strains of "Silent Night"
Echoed with tremolo,
Faith lifted my shuttered window
To prove that it was so.

And there were angels on my porch,
A crescent Christmas choir,
And as they sang my spirits soared
Higher, higher, higher.
They tied a bit of heaven to
The wreath about my door
And left resounding in my heart
Finale of their score.

Magic Tidings

Carol Frye

The hour draws near for the Christmas Eve fete.
The room radiates warmth and good cheer.
'Tis the charmed hour when the symbols speak—
One must pay close attention to hear.

"Joy," sing the scarlet-robed choirboys,
Chanting their musical score.
They carol of laughter and gaiety,
Wishing the world happiness evermore.

"Hope," beam the tall stately candles,
Their flames dancing in a current of air.
Gentle pools of light hold darkness at bay,
Driving out any hint of despair.

"Beauty," whisper the cottony snowflakes
As they sift lazily down from the sky,
Forming a puffy white quilt for the ground,
Concealing barren earth with a sigh.

"Peace," prays the porcelain angel
From her perch at the top of the tree,
Bestowing upon the tableau beneath
A smile of utter serenity.

Finally each message is spoken.
The symbols are all mute save one.
"Love," smiles the mother of the Babe in the straw,
As she fondly looks down on her Son.

Christmas Toys

Edna Jacques

A little dappled horse, a scarlet ball,
A wooly lamb, a doll with sleeping eyes,
A small white angel for a Christmas tree,
A Christmas stocking with a bulky prize.

Red mittens on a string, a pair of skates,
A toy balloon to drift above the house,
Tinsel to glisten in the candlelight,
A little scarlet-coated Mickey Mouse.

A set of dishes for a little girl,
With tiny brier roses here and there,
A locket on a little golden chain,
New patent leather shoes for her to wear.

O crisp December, gay with mistletoe,
Holly and cedar hanging on the door,
Old folks to love, carols to sing in church,
And little children to buy presents for.

Photo Opposite
WINDOW-SHOPPING
H. Armstrong Roberts, Inc.

At Christmastime

Elisabeth Weaver Winstead

Sing a song of Christmas,
Of holly, green and red,
Of icy, windy weather
Just right for skate and sled.

Sing a song of Christmas,
Of candlelight aglow,
Of cookies and plum puddings,
Of freshly fallen snow.

Sing a song of Christmas
As shoppers homeward go,
Of cheery yule logs blazing,
Of stockings in a row.

Sing a song of Christmas,
Star-spangled skies above;
Christmas bells are ringing
Sweet songs of peace and love.

Sing a song of Christmas:
May laughter, love, and cheer
Possess our hearts on Christmas Day
And through a bright New Year.

Scrooge's Resolution

Hilda Butler Farr

"I'm giddy as a schoolboy
Upon a youthful spree;
A merry, merry Christmas!
I'm happy as can be.
What day is this, I wonder . . .
I really do not know
How long I lived with spirits
And wandered to and fro.
And then the bells were ringing
From every church around,
Ding, dong, clash, clang, ding-donging,
Oh, what a merry sound."

So, Scrooge went out walking
And smiled at everyone.
He wished them "Merry Christmas!"
As he had never done.
He went to church and worshipped
With grateful heart indeed,
And talked with little children
And gave to those in need.

Next morning, at the office,
Bob Cratchit came in late,
But Scrooge, of course, was early;
He planned it on this date.
He started first to scold Bob,
As often he would do,
Then changed to "Merry Christmas,"
In a voice that sounded new.
To Bob it was confusing;
He couldn't understand.
But Scrooge was quite in earnest
And clasped him by the hand.

Scrooge was a second father
To Tim, who did not die,
Became the finest master
And friend, as time went by.
He kept the Christmas spirit
Until his years were run . . .
As Tiny Tim re-echoed,
"God bless us every one."

It started with a penny . . . .

In 1907 a ragged newsboy stepped up to the counter where the first Christmas Seals® were being offered and plunked down a penny. He said: "Gimme one. Me sister's got it." He meant tuberculosis, then a raging epidemic.

Today, Christmas Seals® fund the American Lung Association's work to combat all lung diseases.

Photos courtesy of the American Lung Association ®—the Christmas Seal People ®

The First Christmas Seal®

Sophie Knab

It was the first week of December, 1907. Amidst the hustle and bustle of the holiday season, a woman by the name of Emily Bissell was trying to raise three hundred dollars for a small, makeshift hospital on the banks of the Brandywine River in Delaware. All of the patients were suffering from the dreaded killer— tuberculosis—which most people believed left its victims without hope of recovery. The doctors, however, knew that with continued rest and good food tuberculosis patients could be cured. Unfortunately, the money to keep their hospital open was gone. One of the doctors, Emily's cousin, asked her if she could help them. Even though she had no idea how she would do this, she agreed.

While contemplating ways to raise the money, Miss Bissell suddenly remembered a magazine article she had read earlier that year

by a Danish-born reporter named Jacob Riis. He had written about receiving a letter from Denmark with special Christmas stamps stuck all over the envelope. The money raised from the sale of the special stamps had benefited children suffering from tuberculosis.

"Why not have a Christmas stamp to raise money for the hospital?" thought Miss Bissell, and she set to work without delay.

The Delaware Red Cross granted Miss Bissell permission to use the Red Cross emblem. She then drew the design herself—a simple garland of holly around a red cross and the words "Merry Christmas" in a brilliant red color. On December 7, 1907, the first Christmas Seal® sale in America was held in the corridor of the Wilmington, Delaware post office. The stamps sold for a penny apiece.

A Philadelphia newspaper, the *North Ameri-*

can, went into action telling the story of the Christmas Seals®. People began to learn the facts about tuberculosis for the first time. They quickly bought the seals for their Christmas cards and packages. Those who received the cards and gifts were curious about the Christmas Seals® and soon learned their meaning. Each penny stamp became a good-news messenger telling senders and receivers that something could be done about tuberculosis.

Instead of three hundred dollars, the first Christmas Seal Campaign® raised three thousand dollars. The Brandywine hospital was saved. More importantly, a way of fighting tuberculosis had been found. Money from the sale of hundreds of thousands of penny stamps not only helped those who already suffered from the disease, but it also helped to tell others what they could do about the illness.

Like ripples in a pool, the idea of the Christmas Seal® spread rapidly, reaching a popularity and success that extended far beyond its humble origins. The next year the stamps were sold all across America. And in 1920 the red cross on the seal was replaced by a double-barred cross of Lorraine, emblem of the first Crusades, which became the worldwide symbol of the fight against tuberculosis.

This year marks the eighty-first anniversary of the first Christmas Seal®. Since 1919 the Christmas Seal Campaign® has been operated by what is now the American Lung Association. The money still goes to medical research. There can be no doubt that Emily Bissell and her little penny "Merry Christmas" stickers gave the world a great Christmas gift—the opportunity to live a happy, healthy life.

Grandchildren

Cynthia Holt Cummings

Where are the children?
Where have they gone?
I once heard their laughter,
I once heard their song.

There are toys in the attic,
Toys in the hall,
Toys in big boxes,
For children so small.

Bring me the dolls.
Wind up the train.
They're coming home
With children again.

Find the toy soldier,
Once shiny and new.
Bring me the tea set
Of china so blue.

I'll polish the table.
I'll place every chair,
With joy in my heart,
With the children there.

Where are the children?
Where have they gone?
Once more I'll hear laughter,
Once more I'll hear song.

Do You Remember

Garnett Schultz

Do you remember Christmas
Of years so long ago,
The angel on the towering tree,
The candlelight aglow;
And do you still recall the dreams
Of Santa Claus and sleigh,
And how we'd wake before the dawn
When it was Christmas Day?

Do you remember candy canes,
The mistletoe and pine,
The stockings hung so carefully,
The joyous happy time,
The Christmas music soft and low,
The magic organ's sound,
The hush and quiet Christmas Eve,
The secrets all around?

Do you remember yesterday,
Those lovely dreams of yore,
The hearth place with its faces bright,
The wreath upon the door,
The snow that crunched beneath our feet,
And then the warmth of home,
With loving hearts awaiting there
Where gladness was our own?

The gifts and cards, the music gay,
The smell of pumpkin pie,
And cookies every shape and size,
The snow that piled so high,
The treasures of another day,
With peace on earth so dear;
Do you remember all of this
As Christmastime draws near?

Patchwork
Christmas Stocking

Ann Marie Braaten

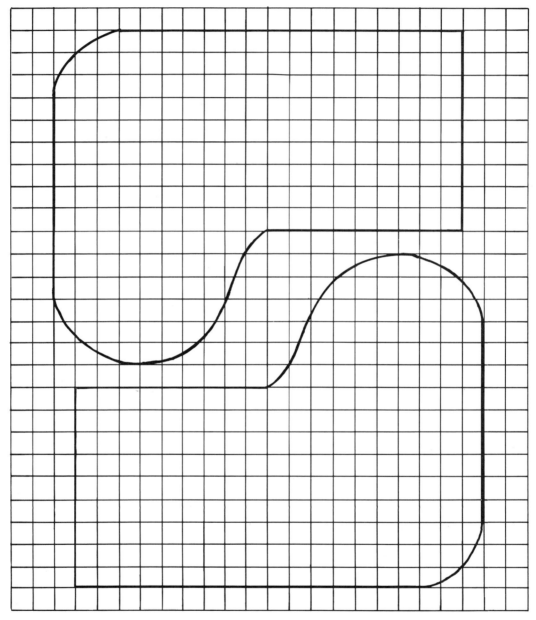

Diagram 1: stocking pattern

Each square equals one inch.

Materials Needed:
¾ yard red print fabric
⅝ yard needle punch
5 remnants of cotton prints in red and green (each
    measuring at least 2 inches by 14 inches)
¾ yard ½-inch-wide ribbon
Matching thread

Construction:
Step One: Cutting

Fold the ¾ yard of red print fabric with selvages together. Lay the stocking pattern on the fabric with the back side of the stocking on the selvage (see diagram 1). Cut two pieces. Position pattern on remaining red fabric. Cut two more pieces for lining.

Cut two stocking pieces from the needle punch.

Cut the five remnant cotton prints into 2-inch by 14-inch strips.

Cut ribbon into two 9-inch pieces and one 6-inch piece.

Step Two: Sewing Patchwork Design

With right sides together, use a ¼-inch seam allowance to sew the five remnant strips together on the long sides (see diagram 2).

From these sewn strips, cut seven 2-inch strips.

Use a ¼-inch seam allowance to sew these patch strips together to form a diagonal design (see diagram 3).

Cut the excess fabric from the patchwork to form a 4½-inch by 9-inch rectangle.

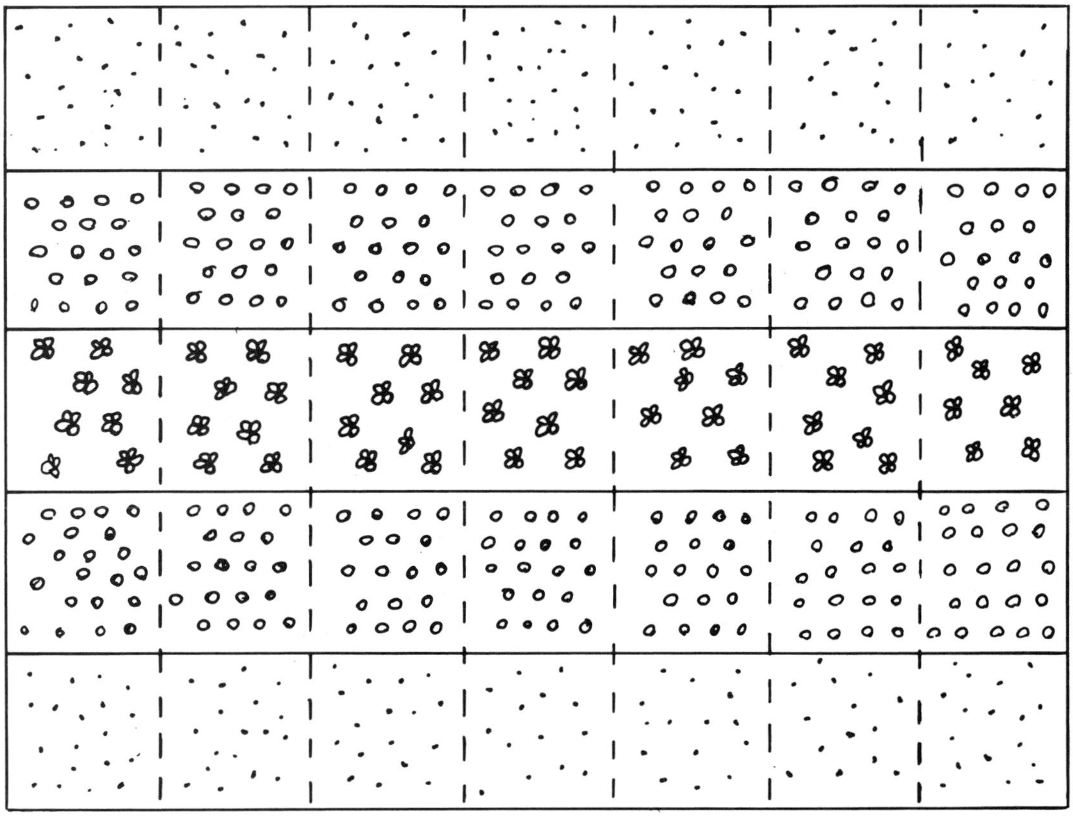

Diagram 2

Cut seven 2-inch strips.

Step Three: Sewing Stocking

With right side up, pin the patchwork rectangle to the stocking front, positioning the top of the patchwork design 1½ inches from the top of the stocking (see photo).

To secure the patchwork to the stocking, sew the 9-inch ribbon pieces along the top and bottom of the patchwork, aligning outer edges of ribbon with outer edges of patchwork.

With right sides together, match stocking front to stocking back. Place needle punch pieces on wrong side of each of these pieces. Using a ½-inch seam allowance, sew through all four layers along the sides and bottom. Leave top of stocking open. Press side seams open. Clip curves. Turn stocking right side out.

With right sides together, match the stocking lining front to the stocking lining back. Using a ½-inch seam allowance, sew along the sides and bottom. Leave top open. Press side seams open. Clip curves.

With right sides together, slip stocking into lining. Use a ½-inch seam allowance to sew around the top edges of the stocking, leaving a 4-inch opening at the back.

Turn stocking and lining to right side. Tuck the lining into the stocking. Slip-stitch back opening closed.

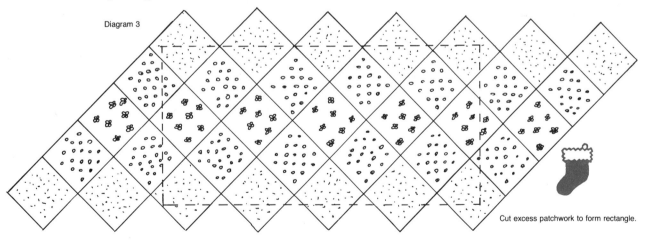

Diagram 3

Cut excess patchwork to form rectangle.

Security

Mary E. Linton

All new trails do hold elements of fear.
Perhaps they should . . . the things we find most dear
Cannot be reached on proven paths and sure.
Unless we have the fiber to endure
And seek our own beyond the first dead end,
Beyond the second or the tenth, and mend
Our broken dreams with hope, what is the choice?
Mute resignation says we have no voice.
What the alternative except retreat?
The seasonless, the lost world of defeat?
Oh, do not ask for certainty to know,
Only for courage, inner power to go
Beyond all doubts, knowing within us lives
The only real security life gives—
Knowing this new path shall not be denied
Through the certain failure of never having tried,
And faith, though this road, too, should prove the same,
To listen when another calls our name.

Photo Opposite
SUGAR HILL CHURCH
NEW HAMPSHIRE
Gene Ahrens Scenic Photographs

Notes of Friendship

Lela Meredith

I treasure all my Christmas cards;
   They mean so much to me,
Each one from someone special whom
   I'd so much like to see.

Some come from friends I don't oft see—
   They live too far away—
Their cards are like a friendly smile
   That brightens Christmas Day.

The message each one brings to me
   From friends on my own street,
Is like a gift that's wrapped with love,
   Each one a yuletide treat.

I'm thankful for these lovely cards
   That come to me each year—
These precious notes of friendship with
   Their greetings of good cheer.

And I wish for you this Christmas all
   The joy the season brings;
Peace, good health, and lots of love—
   The best of everything.

Especially at Christmas

Kay Hoffman

When Christmas comes again
  'Mid holly wreaths and snow,
The precious gift of friendship
  Takes on an added glow.

With each Christmas card we write,
  We see a dear friend's face
And treasure each fond memory
  That time cannot erase.

Though many miles may separate
  Our paths down through the years,
Dear friends are always close at heart
  When Christmastime is here.

Abundant love is tucked inside
  Each Christmas card we send,
And with it there's the silent prayer:
  "God bless you always, friend."

Sunrise Symphony

Nadine Gardner

There beyond my kitchen window,
Singing sweetly in their flight,
Little choristers are gath'ring
In the early morning light.
Perching just above the feeder
On the branches white with snow,
Yellow finches and a nuthatch
Prepare to start the show.

Several sparrows and some bluejays
Harmonize with energy;
To perform his lively solo
Now arrives the chickadee.
A phoebe and a pair of doves
Help to sing the serenade;
So pure a tune, I'm positive
In heaven it was made.

Then come two crimson cardinals,
The husband with his wife,
To lend their voices to the strains
That so enrich my life.
As the sun is slowly climbing
Higher in the eastern sky,
The polyphony diminishes
As singers homeward fly.

And though I dread each ending,
I eternally remain
A faithful fan of feathered friends
Who come to entertain.
So tomorrow at the dawning
Of another day to be,
I'll be listening by my window
For their sunrise symphony.

A Shepherd's Tale

Pamela Kennedy

Andrew walked slowly up the hillside behind the city of Bethlehem. His right hand clutched a shepherd's staff, and his left hand held the gnarled fingers of his blind grandfather, Benjamin. Benjamin had tended the flocks for over forty years, and now that he could no longer see, Andrew, the youngest of his grandsons, was assigned to accompany him to the hills. Day after day and night after night, Andrew had to be his grandfather's eyes, counting and describing the sheep, guiding the old calloused hands over the animals so the seasoned shepherd could assess the condition of his flock.

Benjamin knew every lump and scar on every one of the sheep and told Andrew about each sheep as if it were a favored child. Andrew had heard the stories dozens of times and grew tired of their repetition. He would much rather have been down in the city learning a trade or going to school, but his family was poor, and it had been decided that he would be a shepherd like his grandfather.

Sometimes, though, his grandfather would tell him stories from the scriptures. Andrew never tired of the ancient tales of David and Saul, of Moses and the prophets. He dreamed of being a hero like one of them.

This afternoon, as the sheep grazed and the sun neared the horizon, Benjamin was droning on about Isaiah; how the prophet had said that a great king was coming to rule God's people with justice and truth. Andrew drifted into a dreamless sleep, his head resting on his folded robe.

Benjamin's cry awoke Andrew with a start, and the boy scrambled to his feet, disoriented from sleep and shielding his eyes from the dazzling light that burned in the sky.

"What is it?" the old man whispered in fear.

"I'm not sure," Andrew replied. "It's like the sky is on fire; but there's no heat, just brightness. Oh, Grandfather!"

"What's happening? Tell me, Andrew!"

"I don't know, Grandfather. It looks like people, men in robes, flying in the light."

At that moment, the night was shattered by joyous singing. It was as if the sky had broken in two and music poured out from the heart of the heavens. Chords and harmonies unfamiliar to earthly ears swept around the hillside and lifted the leaves and grasses in a burst of melody. Then words became distinguishable.

Fear not: for, behold, I bring you good tidings of great joy, which shall be to all people. For unto you is born this day in the city of David a Saviour, which is Christ the Lord. And this shall be a sign unto you; Ye shall find the babe wrapped in swaddling clothes, lying in a manger.

Then a chorus began to roll over the hillside like a wave: *"Glory to God in the highest, and on earth peace, good will toward men."* The refrain was repeated again and again until the very rocks echoed it back to the heavens.

Terrified, the shepherds clung to one another. Finally, the voices ceased and the light faded.

"It has happened," Benjamin whispered.

"What has happened?" the others urged.

"He has come. The Messiah has come at last. Oh, praise God!" And Benjamin fell to his knees on the grassy ground.

The others looked at the old man skeptically. Then they began to murmur among themselves, comparing their impressions of the astonishing event they had just witnessed. Finally, one of them spoke with conviction. "I think we should go and see this thing."

"But how do we know where to go?" asked another.

"The angel said the child would be in a manger," Benjamin said, "wrapped in cloth and lying in a manger in Bethlehem. It is just as the prophets have written!"

"Come, Andrew, give me your hand."

Andrew obeyed his grandfather with reluctance, fearful of the things he had just seen and heard and suddenly fearful of the old man who seemed to understand it all.

As the two started down the hillside, the others followed, whispering among themselves.

Thus they traveled through the darkened streets of Bethlehem, Benjamin navigating as if led by some inner compass.

Before long, they came to a small inn which appeared to be locked and shuttered for the night. Benjamin whispered to his grandson, "Come, it is here."

Skirting the building, the little group of shepherds approached the rocky, cave-like stable at the back. Pushing past several tethered donkeys, some sleepy cows, and a few restless sheep, they came upon a startled couple, kneeling in the straw. The woman reached protectively for a tiny bundle that was resting in a stone manger.

Falling to his knees again, Benjamin spoke to the couple he could not see. "We have come to worship the Messiah. Is it as Isaiah has said: 'Behold, a virgin shall conceive, and bear a son, and shall call him Immanuel'?"

Andrew watched the young mother as her eyes warmed with understanding at the old man's words. Gently, she lowered the infant into the old man's arms, and Andrew saw his grandfather's body tremble at the touch of the tiny babe.

"It is he," the mother whispered, and tears slipped from the sightless eyes as Benjamin held the hope of Israel against his breast.

Later, Andrew could not recall how long they had lingered in the stable. Time seemed to have little meaning that night. But what he did recall was the lighter step of his grandfather as they returned to the hills. No one spoke as they settled back onto the familiar rocks and wrapped their robes about them to stop the chill.

But when the rosy pink of dawn slipped up the morning sky, Benjamin broke the stillness.

"Andrew," he said with wonder, "bring me that newborn lamb," and, extending one trembling hand to point, he added, "the one to the right of the olive tree there."

The Song of Christmas

Gail Brook Burket

When joyous words the angel choirs
First sang to watching men
Sound sweetly on the frosty air
Of Christmas Eve again,

May they awake the fervent awe
And hushed humility
Lone shepherds knew the radiant night
Of Christ's nativity.

And every heart which is attuned
To that celestial song
Will find it holds the joyous hope
For which all people long.

Then will new faith and love replace
Old darkness put to flight,
And glory light the blessed earth
As on that holy night.

Photo Opposite
SILENT NIGHT
Bill Hebden Stock Photographs

The Christmas Story

And it came to pass in those days, that there went out a decree from Caesar Augustus, that all the world should be taxed. (And this taxing was first made when Cyrenius was governor of Syria.) And all went to be taxed, every one into his own city. And Joseph also went up from Galilee, out of the city of Nazareth, into Judaea, unto the city of David, which is called Bethlehem; (because he was of the house and lineage of David:) To be taxed with Mary his espoused wife, being great with child. And so it was, that, while they were there, the days were accomplished that she should be delivered. And she brought forth her firstborn son, and wrapped him in swaddling clothes, and laid him in a manger; because there was no room for them in the inn. And there were in the same country shepherds abiding in the field, keeping watch over their flock by night. And, lo, the angel of the Lord came upon them, and the glory of the Lord shone round about them: and they were sore afraid. And the angel said unto them, *Fear not: for, behold, I bring you good tidings of great joy, which shall be to all people. For unto you is born this day in the city of David a Saviour, which is Christ the Lord. And this shall be a sign unto you; Ye shall find the babe wrapped in swaddling clothes, lying in a manger.* And suddenly there was with the angel a multitude of the heavenly host praising God, and saying, *Glory to God in the highest, and on earth peace, good will toward men*. And it came to pass, as the angels were gone away from them into heaven, the shepherds said one to another, *Let us now go even unto Bethlehem, and see this thing which is come to pass, which the Lord hath made known unto us*. And they came with haste, and found Mary, and Joseph, and the babe lying in a manger. And when they had seen it, they made known abroad the saying which was told them concerning this child. And all they that heard it wondered at those things which were told them by the shepherds. But Mary kept all these things, and pondered them in her heart. And the shepherds returned, glorifying and praising God for all the things that they had heard and seen, as it was told unto them.

Luke 2:1-20

In His Place

Emalu Byrd

The Christmas holiday season was fast approaching and the stepped-up activity within the classroom could be seen and felt. As the children busily made decorations for the room after their assigned lessons were done, one could hear the cheerful, quiet humming of the carols that they had been learning in their music class. I sat at my desk, stapling together the red and green decorations that had been carefully, if crudely, cut and glued. I glanced at the crèche on the back bookcase, and . . . I saw that it had happened again: the baby Jesus was missing.

The crèche was an old one. I had bought it years before in a department store basement. The crèche was also a simple one. Only baby Jesus was movable. Mary, Joseph, a shepherd, and one white sheep were fastened to the floor of the stable. Interestingly, each year, in this room to which five- and six-year-old children come, the baby Jesus disappeared. But, even more interestingly, he always reappeared as the holiday drew closer.

As I mused about this, Dallas got up from his chair and took a circuitous route to the waste-basket with a crumpled piece of colored paper. When he started back to his desk, I saw him pause in front of the crèche, reach into his pocket, and take from it what I knew by this time to be the Christ Child figure. Using both little hands, he placed it carefully in the simple manger and patted it lightly and lovingly. Then he skipped to his seat, slid to a sudden stop, sat down, and started cutting again, smiling a radiant smile and breaking into a gusty humming of "Away in a Manger."

I smiled. I knew that Dallas had taught me a lesson in the busy room that day. When we put the Christ Child in his rightful place in our lives, all is well. We are truly filled with joy!

The Lasting Gifts

Garnett Schultz

So many times dear ones will ask
What would you like this day,
And what would bring you Christmas joy
That I might give away?
A question posed a hundred times,
And yet we do forget
The treasures that would mean the most,
The dearest gifts to get.

Expectancy—rich happiness,
Good health that means so much,
Undying faith in God above,
A loved one's tender touch,
A peace of mind—a happy heart,
A confidence serene,
A worthwhile thought to live and grow,
A lovely lasting dream.

These are the gifts—the lasting gifts—
To treasure through the years,
A zest for living each new day,
A smile instead of fears.
What would you like this Christmas Day?
So much we all possess;
Abundantly our God gives all
In lasting happiness.

What Do I Want

Mrs. Paul E. King

What do I want for Christmas,
And what does my heart most desire?
The warmth and worth of true friendship,
A neighborly chat by the fire;
The wealth of a small child's laughter
And his trusting fingers round mine . . .
Just give me these blessings for Christmas
And the presents may all be thine.

What do I want for Christmas
And what does my heart ask for me?
The privilege of living for others,
Like the Christ Child, unselfishly.
The wealth of seeing a morning
All golden with warm sunshine . . .
Just give me these blessings for Christmas
And the presents may all be thine.

What do I want for Christmas?
Gifts of deeper worth
Than those adorned with tinsel
And signed with wit or mirth;
Gifts, like dew of the morning,
To fall into this life of mine . . .
Just give me these daily blessings
And the presents may all be thine.

The Christmas Bell

Margaret Rorke

I heard a bell on Christmas Day
Speak out in such a holy way
I paused to hear what it might say.

In tones resounding ancient pride
It tolled of that first Christmastide,
Of Joseph and his virgin bride.

It said the newborn could not sleep.
Though in his mother's gentle keep,
He somehow couldn't help but weep.

And then he heard a tinkling bell
That had the power to soothe and tell
The infant Christ that all was well.

None knows just where the bell was hung
Or by whose hands its cord was rung,
But all bells praise its sacred tongue.

Our God, thus pleased, sought not the where
Of that small tinkle in the air,
But let all bells its blessing share.

To them—the big and very small—
He gave life's purest, sweetest call:
"A Merry Christmas—one and all!"

Photo Opposite
CHRISTMAS BELLS
Al Riccio

Voices in the Mist

Alfred, Lord Tennyson

The time draws near the birth of Christ:
　　The moon is hid; the night is still;
　　The Christmas bells from hill to hill
Answer each other in the mist.

Four voices of four hamlets round,
　　From far and near, on mead and moor,
　　Swell out and fail, as if a door
Were shut between me and the sound:

Each voice four changes on the wind,
　　That now dilate, and now decrease,
　　Peace and goodwill, goodwill and peace,
Peace and goodwill, to all mankind.

White Lace

Ruth Alla Wager

Go, walk in soft, white lace
Along the streets of town
And feel the caressing flakes
Of snow as they fall down.

Tall pine trees primly stand
Adorned in gowns of white,
Placed by a gentle hand
Through dark hours of the night.

The snowflakes still pile high,
Covering branches bare;
As you are passing by
You'll want to stand and stare

At yards of soft, white lace,
At trees in grand array,
And in the soundless space
You'll find beauty for today.

A Slice of Life

Edgar A. Guest

The story of an opportunity has always fascinated me. At Christmastime I always think of the people whose privilege it was to play a part in the glory of Bethlehem. I sympathize greatly with the innkeeper there. His was a golden opportunity which he never sensed.

I fancy that innkeepers then were much like innkeepers now. They have their problems and their troubles, and their inns become crowded, and guests at times must be turned away. I can imagine Joseph and Mary arriving at the crowded hostel and being told that there was no room for them. He must have had sympathy in his breast, for he realized Mary's condition and offered her the stable. He never knew the miracle of that birth. I doubt that he ever lived to know that his inn and his stable and his act would be remembered and recalled through all the ages so long as this world shall exist.

Someday I fancy I shall meet him over there. A friend may introduce him as the innkeeper at Bethlehem, and I think I know exactly what he will say to me—I have heard it said so often here on earth—"If I had known that he was a friend, I might have found room for him." By letters of introduction, men today contrive to get accommodations which to total strangers are coldly denied. This is only human. Men always have and always will favor the well known. It is as natural that it should have happened then as that it happens now.

And so, if we ever shall meet and I shall ask that innkeeper about that first Christmas Eve at Bethlehem, I am sure he will shake his head and say: "If only I had known." Of course, he will regret it, but there never comes a Christmas Eve but what I think of him.

"Oh, if only I had known!"
    Said the keeper of the inn.
"But no hint to me was shown,
    And I didn't let them in.

"Yes, a star gleamed overhead,
    But I couldn't read the skies,
And I'd given every bed
    To the very rich and wise.

"And she was so poorly clad,
    And he hadn't much to say!
But no room for them I had,
    So I ordered them away.

"She seemed tired, and it was late
    And they begged so hard, that I,
Feeling sorry for her state,
    In the stable let them lie.

"Had I turned some rich man out
    Just to make a place for them,
'Twould have killed, beyond a doubt,
    All my trade at Bethlehem.

"Then there came the wise men three
    To the stable, with the morn,
Who announced they'd come to see
    The great King who had been born.

"And they brought Him gifts of myrrh
    Costly frankincense and gold,
And a great light shone on her
    In the stable, bleak and cold.

"All my patrons now are dead
    And forgotten, but today
All the world to peace is led
    By the ones I sent away.

"It was my unlucky fate
    To be born that inn to own,
Against Christ I shut my gate—
    Oh, if only I had known!"

Keeping Christmas

Henry Van Dyke

It is a good thing to observe Christmas Day.
The mere marking of times and seasons, when men agree to stop work
and make merry together, is a wise and wholesome custom.
It helps one to feel the supremacy of the common life over the individual life.
It reminds a man to set his own little watch, now and then,
by the great clock of humanity which runs on sun time.
But there is a better thing than the observance of Christmas Day,
and that is keeping Christmas.
Are you willing to forget what you have done for other people,
and to remember what other people have done for you;
to ignore what the world owes you, and to think what you owe the world;
to put your rights in the background, and your duties in the middle distance,
and your chances to do a little more than your duty in the foreground;
to see that your fellowmen are just as real as you are,
and try to look behind their faces to their hearts hungry for joy;
to own that probably the only good reason for your existence
is not what you are going to get out of life, but what you are going to give to life;
to close your book of complaints against the management of the universe,
and look around you for a place where you can sow a few seeds of happiness—
are you willing to do these things even for a day?
Then you can keep Christmas.
Are you willing to stoop down and consider the needs and the desires of little children;
to remember the weakness and loneliness of people who are growing old;
to stop asking how much your friends love you,
and ask yourself whether you love them enough;
to bear in mind the things that other people have to bear in their hearts;
to try to understand what those who live in the same house with you really want,
without waiting for them to tell you;
to trim your lamp so that it will give more light and less smoke,
and to carry it in front so that your shadow will fall behind you;
to make a grave for your ugly thoughts and a garden for your kindly feelings,
with the gate open—
are you willing to do these things even for a day?
Then you can keep Christmas.
Are you willing to believe that love is the strongest thing in the world—
stronger than hate, stronger than evil, stronger than death—
and that the blessed life which began in Bethlehem nineteen hundred years ago
is the image and brightness of the Eternal Love?
Then you can keep Christmas,
And if you can keep it for a day, why not always?
But you can never keep it alone.

Photo Opposite
LAMPLIGHT WELCOME
Henry J. Hupp
Laatsch-Hupp Photo

The Twenty-Sixth of December

Dr. Donald R. Stoltz

Christmas Eve is memory,
   And Christmas Day has gone,
And now a new December—
The twenty-sixth—has dawned.
The holiday is over,
The year is history,
And the only vivid evidence
Is a tinseled Christmas tree.

The kids have all their presents;
Now they're nowhere to be seen,
And slowly people everywhere
Are returning to routine.
There are no voices caroling;
There are no sounds of fun.
The world just seems a bit depressed
'Cause Christmas is all done.

And in a place so far away
Rests a man with strength depleted,
For as everyone returns to work
His job is now completed.
He slumps into his favorite chair,
Too weak to get undressed,
His fur-lined boots kicked off to give
His weary feet a rest.

He has traveled to so many lands
With his reindeer and his sleigh
And has spread the Christmas spirit
As he coursed along his way.
He has driven through great blizzards
And has fought the tropic sun
As he circumnavigated earth,
Bringing pleasure, gifts, and fun.

And now his journey is complete;
He's earned a nice long rest,
And soon his head droops in deep sleep
With his beard upon his chest.
And as he dreams, he recollects
The centuries gone by
And the many miles he has flown
Across the winter sky,

And the happy faces he has seen
And the laughter and the joys,
And the tons of presents he has brought
To countless girls and boys.
And now it's slumber, well deserved,
Without a doubt or fear.
Then when he wakes, he will begin
Preparing for next year.

So children everywhere, take note,
When you're feeling very glum,
'Cause Christmas Eve has come and gone
And Christmas Day is done;
Just remember what this day is
And you'll feel a new elation,
For on December twenty-sixth,
Santa Claus takes his vacation.

Lines on a Snowy Night

Virginia Mathson Carlson

There's no more peaceful sight I know
Than my world filling up with snow;
Than viewing on a quiet night
A landscape wrapped in winter white,
With snowflakes falling thick and dense,
Clothing the earth in innocence.

I wish that all could share with me
This moment of tranquillity;
Could feel flakes brush across their face
Like fragments of transparent lace,
And love the whispering wind that shifts
Snow cargoes into softest drifts.

I sense a sheer echantment grow
Within this white, hushed world of snow,
And feel on such a night that I
Am kin to all of earth and sky;
Knowing that surely I must be
Chief heir to God's infinity.

Photo Opposite
SNOW-COVERED FARMSTEAD
Ken Dequaine

Ring Out, Wild Bells

Alfred, Lord Tennyson

Ring out, wild bells, to the wild sky,
 The flying cloud, the frosty light:
 The year is dying in the night;
Ring out, wild bells, and let him die.

Ring out the old, ring in the new,
 Ring, happy bells, across the snow:
 The year is going, let him go;
Ring out the false, ring in the true.

Ring out the grief that saps the mind,
 For those that here we see no more;
 Ring out the feud of rich and poor,
Ring in redress to all mankind.

Ring out a slowly dying cause,
    And ancient forms of party strife;
    Ring in the nobler modes of life,
With sweeter manners, purer laws.

Ring out the want, the care, the sin,
    The faithless coldness of the times;
    Ring out, ring out my mournful rhymes,
But ring the fuller minstrel in.

Ring out false pride in place and blood,
    The civic slander and the spite;
    Ring in the love of truth and right,
Ring in the common love of good.

Ring out old shapes of foul disease;
    Ring out the narrowing lust of gold;
    Ring out the thousand wars of old,
Ring in the thousand years of peace.

Ring in the valiant man and free,
    The larger heart, the kindlier hand;
    Ring out the darkness of the land,
Ring in the Christ that is to be.

Merry
Christmas
from all of
us at

ideals®

ACKNOWLEDGMENTS

MISSED OPPORTUNITIES from *EDGAR A. GUEST BROADCASTING,* copyright 1935, The Reilly & Lee Co. Used by permission; CHRISTMAS TOYS by Edna Jacques from *ROSES IN DECEMBER,* copyright 1944 and 1952 by Thomas Allen Publishers, Ltd., Ontario, CAN. Used by permission; KEEPING CHRISTMAS by Henry van Dyke from *SPIRIT OF CHRISTMAS,* copyright 1905 by Charles Scribner's Sons. Our sincere thanks to the following whose addresses we were unable to locate: Beatrice Branch for CHRISTMAS IN FLORIDA; Virginia Mathson Carlson for LINES ON A SNOWY NIGHT; Cynthia Holt Cummings for GRANDCHILDREN; Helen Fahrbach for WINTER FISHING; Carol Frye for MAGIC TIDINGS; George W. Goretzke for SIGNS BEFORE CHRISTMAS; Ada Mae Hoffrek for WINTER COUNTRYSIDE; Ruth Alla Wager for WHITE LACE.